Prayers for Unfolding Ultimate Health:

Principles of Divine Healing

by Marshall L. Davis

Spiritual Guidance Society Publications
181 NW 23 Avenue, Pompano Beach, FL 33069
sgsocietypub.com

copyright ©2012 Marshall L. Davis

Prayers for Unfolding Ultimate Health:
Principles of Divine Healing
Published by Spiritual Guidance Society Publications
181 NW 23 Avenue
Pompano Beach, FL 33069
sgsocietypub.com

Edited by BluestockingInc Limited

All rights reserved. No part of this book may be reproduced, stored in a retrieval system, or transmitted, in any form or by any means, electronic, mechanical, photocopying, recording, or otherwise, without the written permission of the author.

ISBN: 978-1-937701-00-0

Library of Congress Control Number: 2011938308
Library of Congress subject headings
Prayers
Affirmations
Spiritual life
Religion
Hope—Prayers and devotions
Mental healing
Self-care, Health
Christianity and yoga
Visualization—Therapeutic use

Prayers for Unfolding Ultimate Health: Principles of Divine Healing

Table of Contents

HEALING YOURSELF & OTHERS I
    INTRODUCTION I
DECREE OF HEALTH AND HEALING 1
    VERSE 1 2
    VERSE 2: 4
    VERSE 3: 6
    VERSE 4: 7
    VERSE 5: 9
        SEVEN ARCHANGLES *11*
    VERSE 6: 12
    VERSE 7: 14
    VERSE 8: 15
    VERSE 9: 20
    VERSE 10: 21
THE TEMPLE OF THE INDWELLING CHRIST 23
    VERSE 1: 25
    VERSE 2: 27
    VERSE 3: 28
    VERSE 4: 32
    VERSE 5: 35
HEALING LIGHT 37
    LET THERE BE LIGHT! 39
    THE SPECTRUM OF LIGHT 41
    SPIRITUAL ENERGY CENTERS OF CONSCIOUS 44
        SPIRITUAL CENTERS 45
    THE TRUE LIGHT OF BEING 46
        FIVE SPIRITUAL BREATH *47*
    THE KINGOM OF GOD INFINITE LIVING LIGHT 48
        The realms of the Kingdom of GOD are characterized by the elements: *51*

HEALING YOURSELF & OTHERS

BY MARSHALL L. DAVIS

INTRODUCTION

Health is a state of life and not just a condition of the physical body. True healing is the processes that are used to restore holistic health. This is to say, it brings balance and order to the physical, the emotional, and the mental aspects of man who has been dis-eased or unbalanced and out of harmonious order. Health is a restoration, right alignment and re-integration of the individual composite being into oneness with divinity.

This book was not written to focus on any one method of healing, especially as it relates to the physical body. There are numerous books written on various methods, some of which are described herein. Rather, this text came about to share and provide eternal wisdom principles and affirmations of truths that will aid you, as a sincere practitioner, to obtain and sustain health. It is hoped that you will find these truth affirmations, spiritual treatments and principles enlightening and empowering to your existence and development. I prayed that truth aids you in achieving ultimate health for your bodies—physical, astral, ethereal, and mental—while obtaining freedom for your soul. Ultimate health is needed on a planet of ill and sickened individuals, who in such unbalanced conditions of body, emotions, and mental matrix have infected each other with untold horrors, illusions and un-godliness.

The enlightenment suggested herein will not come from simply reading the empowering truth, but requires that you will unlearn concepts that are false, and will apply the principles in your thoughts, words and actions during prayers, mediations, affirmations and right living. For many, healing, enlightenment and empowerment come as a gradual process. That is a pre-requisite for most living things, for others it will be a transformation that occurs in the twinkling of an eye.

To achieve the lofty goal of holistic health, you must have an understanding of God and self. It is no doubt that there are many methods of healing—medical and metaphysical, organic and mechanical, pranic and surgical, exercises and visualizations, etc.—in which you might engage and find beneficial. Those in need of such support should avail themselves of the solutions that conforms to their state of being or need. Too often individuals have attempted to conform to methods that they, in their compromised condition and state of soul existence, are not prepared to benefit from, regardless of their belief system. Such individuals have not risen to the level of faith [conscious certainty & intuitive knowing] that they will activate the divine qualities of their souls. Based on the state and faith of the individual, Jesus himself used various means and methods to heal and to release the needy of malicious entities.

Healing in its highest form is divine. When healing is truly divine, it is complete in body, mind and soul. Divine healing unlike all others methods—mental, metaphysical, spiritual, dietary, etc.—eliminates the cause of the inharmony and restores one to the full measure of complete health in each aspect of the individual. It aligns you with divine purpose and pure practical application of the truth.

Divine healing like any divine intervention is an initiatory experience that is vital and vibrant to you unfolding your soul qualities. The truth herein is given to enlighten you regarding the truth of your being, the causal factors that lead to illnesses, and the fallen condition of mankind. It is also given to provide methods and concepts predicated on truth that will enable you to engage successfully in the healing of yourself and others.

Decree of Health and Healing

The Light of God is the divine x-ray to my physical, ethereal, astral and mental bodies.

Divine Wisdom, which created, formed and made me, is the power that heals and restores me to perfect health.

Divine intelligence reveals the cause of the hidden condition, as well as the treatment necessary to eradicate the effects at its source.

God's prescription and treatment is a whole plan of action that results in balance and order within my composite being.

With loving-kindness the angels that heal injuries and eliminate diseases, on every level of my existence, administer their healing rays to restore my health and wellbeing.

In the light of God's healing power my strength of being and purpose are invigorated and I radiate joy and confidence in living a life of vitality and virtue.

My health is nurtured with love and maintained by remaining steadfast to God's perfect plan, divine truth and worthy goals.

Through Christ I release stress and develop my health by exercising by being with sincere prayer, positive thinking, affirmations of truth, meditations, noble deeds, supportive acts of charity, spiritual treatments, beneficial physical exercise and wholesome holy living.

I immerse myself in the healing rays of Christ and radiate the light of health to those I meet on the pathway of life.

Christ is the authority that emanates health and healing within me and is a living flame that shields me from every form of sickness, disease, disorder and danger.

DECREE OF HEALTH AND HEALING
COMMENTARY

Verse 1

The Light of God is the divine x-ray to my physical, ethereal, astral and mental bodies.

The existence of man as with all things is on several levels. The most conscious and acceptable existence of man for the masses is the physical state of being. However there are other states of existence, whether one is conscious of these non-physical or metaphysical realities, or not. These metaphysical states are identified by various theological terms such as the astral body, according to eastern traditions, or the nephesh–animal soul and the ruach–form being (Formed Adam), according to other traditions. These terms are means to identify and clarify the emotional aspect of one's being. The mental body is known as the mana in Hindu, the mind in Western psychology, or neshema in kabbalah. These are terms used as means to evaluate the function of the mental body or mental self. The functions or operations of the mental body, i.e. the consciousness, sub-consciousness, unconsciousness and super-consciousness, are often themselves distinguished as entities that can be in opposition to each other.

Everyone and everything has a composite existence. This multiple existence, like all life, is a symbiotic relationship. Although one has multi-existence that function in the various realms according to divinity, the divine plan is to operate in unity while harmoniously integrating and regulating the aspects of self and the *centers of consciousness and energy* (i.e. the chakras). When that which we call dis-ease, illness or sickness manifest it is a result of some imbalance and/or dis-integration. It may be an invasion or acceptance of some entity or property that is adverse and malefic to one's well-being. Indeed some diseases are grown and gestate from the substance and form of ill conceived thoughts and emotions.

The inappropriate balance and disarrayed consciousness/energy centers can be found in the aspects of self, which must be purified and corrected in order to obtain and sustain health.

The aspects of self or the individual that is out of balance can be either singularly or collectively in the mental body, the astral body or the physical body. The health of each aspect depends on how it is appropriately and sufficiently fed and exercised, as well as, how it is restricted and restored. This affirmation is to confirm, accept and cooperate with the principles of health.

It is placing one's entire being under the examination of the hierarchy of heaven to discover and rightly discern the cause of the mal-condition(s) and to achieve the appropriate cure by uprooting that which causes the manifestation of the disease. Rather than pacify the seeds of sickness with erroneous perceptions, acidic attitudes, feel-good drugs and other means that remedy nothing, it encourages and affirms the application of health principles to increase and sustain radiant health.

The first verse engages the principle of light to exam and to reveal that which is known and unknown, that is, what is the causative factor for the manifestation of the ill condition. The principle of light is the source of the life energy that can produce healing directly, if one is receptive to and able to manage its fusion on such a high level.

Light is the essence and is essential to life, while life energy/substance is essential to health. The essentials of physical health are the elements of life. Elements are the products of life energy. These essentials elements are depicted as the elements know as fire, air, water, and earth. Each of the elements is a manifestation of ether (life energy/substance), vibrating at a rate that results in the characteristic of either fire, air, water, or earth. The truth student should understand that each of these elements exist in the other metaphysical realms.

Light is truly Emmanuel, God with us. God is the essence of our divine being. In him was life and the life was the light of men. (John 1:4)

Verse 2:

Divine Wisdom, which created formed and made me, is the power that heals and restores me to perfect health.

The entity known as man (Adam), according to the Hebrew Holy Scripture, was *created*, then *formed*, and thereafter *made*. The accounting of these *states* of man is not only to indicate his composite existence but also the realms of existence in which man dwells consciously or unknowingly.

God created man in his image; formed him from the dust (participles of light) in the realm of formation (the astral earth). The *fall*, the *shame, or, the impaling light of the entity-man, was the exiting of the higher vibratory divine nature from man's being. This impaling of the vibratory light of the entity-man resulted in his decent to a lower vibratory physical world where "they" were provided* with *"coats of skin"* and became, to a greater degree, an entity imposed upon by the acquired physical sheath.

The beings known as man (Adam) were dismissed from the higher realm into physical existence (involution of the soul into matter) without the fused connection of the higher vibratory light that was once a state of their existence, as well as an integral part of their being. This involution of the *disintegrated soul being* into matter marks the promised death cycle: separation from the higher soul nature.

Like the *creation of man (Adam)*, the *process of manifestation* is initiated with the *sacred divine name (nature, power, principle or state)* of the Holy One—blessed be the omnific name. This process then creates within the realm of creation, forms within the realm of formation, and subsequently expresses its manifestation through the world of physical action where things evolve and are made and transmute.

This process is a means to undergo regeneration of the health that is desirable, whereby one in wisdom can ascend the ladder of light to heaven, and/or obtain from heaven's sanctuary the essence of light that is the life energy/substance required for restoration. Perfect health is complete health. It is the life energy/substance regulated within all the states of one's being reaching optimum level. Perfect health is the synchronization of each aspect of the entity-man with the image and likeness designed and purposed by God. It is the reintegration and balanced state of the inner life force.

The wisdom, love, and power of the Holy Breath is one of the most effective yet overlooked means to restore, maintain, and create health and healing energies. It was the breath (*neshema*) of life (*chayah*) disseminated or spirited (*breathed ruach*) into the **dust-formed entity-man** by God (*Elohim*) that resulted in the **formed man-entity** becoming a living soul.

The air we breathe typifies this process of the essential aspects and need for the Holy Breath. The three essential breath sequences are the intake of breath, the sustained breath, and the exhaled breath. Inhalation corresponds to the feminine lunar breath known in *kundalini* yoga as the *ida* flow. The exhalation represents the masculine solar breath called *pingala*. The sustained breath in the physical, which energizes and eliminates, represents the creative breath known in the yoga system as the *shushumna*.

Beyond the science known and unknown to modern man, and the treatments revealed and unrevealed, Divine Wisdom can heal. However, it must be realized that sustained health is preferred above healing. The methods of healing and the issue of "if" one will be healed, are not solely in the hands of medical doctors, healers, angels, or heaven. We must accept responsibility for our state of existence. Many have taken the same medications, undergone the same surgery, experienced the same process or treatment, been prayed for by the same healer, yet some respond favorably and the others do not. Jesus healed numerous people, but others, such as those in his own home, were not receptive to his restoring touch. There are many variables involved when one is not healed. A person's faith, will to live, the faith of the healer, the prayers of the faithful, the preponderance of negative thoughts (worry, fears, despair, etc.), the negative or wicked wishes and acts of others, the skills of the doctor, the cosmos, the time and day, and the individual's karma are just a few examples. Applied wisdom can overcome them all, when it is wise to do so.

Verse 3:

Divine intelligence reveals the cause of the hidden condition, as well as the treatment necessary to eradicate the effects at its source.

When man understands that the condition of his health is related to the state and condition of his mind, emotions, experiences, and environment, he will possess a better ability to avoid illnesses and become more consistently healed. When one unifies his soul, mind, and body with divinity, and properly aligns the inner creative energies, he or she can indeed be healed and grow to become a healer of others.

Man has amassed a plethora of knowledge and understanding regarding the arts and sciences of disease and medicine, and nutrition and health. The restoration of the individual is not sustained by the degree that one makes intelligent use of such misdirected knowledge. This includes a spiritually enlightened understanding of divine principles and life's purpose, putting the right applications into practice, and medical practices and/or treatments that will affect a cure or a healing. The healer does not go without blame for the misuse of knowledge acquired or ignored, be it scientific or theological.

Suffering and sickness will continue to plague our existence and experiences, until medical practices are such that they do not harm and that they cease vain, selfish endeavors and wicked works. Many of our medical achievements are, have been, and will continue to be polluted by "the knowledge of good and evil" and thereby lack the pure influence of the ***Tree of Life.***

Eradication of diseases at the source is the most intelligent approach and solution to the restoration of health. The purging of malefic thinking, emotions, desires, and addictive behavior is the inner task to improving one's health and character. Improving the inner constitution and the matrix of thoughts and emotions, while aligning the same with principles of truth and life, are essential to one's health and spiritual unfolding. Thoughts and emotions of our making become either angelic or demonic entities (i.e., thought-forms, emotional-forms) that support or become detrimental to our wellbeing.

There are viable physical means available to aid one in discovering his or her internal physical state, such as x-rays, magnetic scans, analysis of the blood, hair, or other body specimens. Asian practitioners possess a long history of success with nontraditional methods when compared to treatments and customs practiced in Western medicine. Metaphysical interpretation or analysis of physical phenomenal by means such as iridology, the Vedic arts of phrenology, oriental or Hebrew palmistry, *Feng Shui*, Taoist methods (including pulse reading, tongue analysis, and/or other methods unfamiliar to Western medical traditions) could be of significant usefulness.

Verse 4:

God's prescription and treatment is a whole plan of action that results in balance and order within my composite being.

There are various medical procedures that are too strenuous for some patients to undergo. While some medications are helpful in controlling symptoms for some patients, they can be detrimental and even deadly to others. Indeed a number of practices and procedures may be unnecessarily prescribed just because it is the surgical or medical specialty of the doctor. It also needs to be noted that because one has the scientific knowledge or means to perform certain procedures or provide certain medications–whether calling it science, an individual's intellectual rights, or a viable medical practice–does not mean that it is in accordance with divine purpose and true health. This holds particularly true if the method or medication employed does not restore, cure, heal, and/or serve as beneficial to one's wellbeing (karma).

Medication becomes an inescapable daily regiment for many. And it is of great concern that many medications prescribed to support, relieve, or cure an ailment can become addictive. Any treatment, surgical and nonsurgical procedures, medication, etc. that creates malefic-karma and grave imbalance ought not to be supported, and by all means necessary, avoided. This is a matter of choice and quality of living wherein one has the right to select and choose wisely. In order to make a wise choice, one must be cognizant of the available viable alternatives. Natural, organic nutrition and treatments are deserving of diligent research. Natural food for a natural body makes sense. Discovering the foods that will sustain health and endow healing, how to prepare them, and the combinations of the food types, is well deserving of research. Included in nutritional value thinking is the necessity of cleaning the excretory systems and boosting the immune system. The benefits of accomplishing this goal is worthy of investigation. But the herbs, fasting methods, and other means to achieve a clean internal system must be suitable for the individual.

The individual should consider the nature of food as predicated by the four elements–fire, earth, air and water–as well as yang-masculine or yin-feminine principles. The polarity or gender of food sources has a significant effect on the type of energy of the individual's physical body. It also has an effect on the individual's mental state, emotional disposition, and character. While yang-type foods support and strengthen one's assertive nature, yin-type foods aid one in becoming tranquil and sedate.

Some major concerns deserving close scrutiny as it relates to protecting one's health are the genetic altering of foods, and the use of herbicides and pesticides. The treatment approach that regards health as if it is not only of the body, but addresses other aspects of man's composite-existence, is called (w)holistic. The whole plan of action for health is inclusive of one's environment, cultural experiences, nutritional plan, emotional and mental wellbeing, as well as attunement with spiritual aspects.

Verse 5:

With loving-kindness the angels that heal injuries and eliminate diseases, on every level of my existence, administer their healing rays to restore my health and wellbeing.

One of the most noted Archangels of health is Raphael (meaning God heals). In truth, every angel provides some aspect of healing and restoration to life's purposes of **health, happiness, harmony** and **Holiness**. Whether our health issues include a deficiency or excess within the physical system, balance can be restored with angelic services. Angels can guide us to the nutritional foods or supplements and treatment needed to improve health. "He will give his angels charge over thee to keep thee in all thy ways" (Psalms 91:11). In every noble and worthy endeavor of life there are angels available and assigned to help. There are also demonic entities ever ready to instigate and aid in conditioning negativity.

The symbiotic relationship we have with the angels of the hierarchy of heaven is on both the microcosmic and macrocosmic levels. This symbiotic relationship, on the microscopic level, involves angels that deal with the innate intelligent design and life energy of cells, molecules, DNA, atoms (and its protons, neutrons, and electrons), as well as the quarks in quantum physics in the physical existence. Other angelic entities are those that serve and minister to us in ways that affect and improve us emotionally, psychically, mentally, and spiritually.

In cooperating with the angelic hierarchy of heaven we should remember Paul's key statements regarding: "our reasonable service," (Romans 12:1) "be careful how we entertain strangers in that we may be unaware that we're entertaining angels," (Hebrews 13:2) and in the latter days, some would get into deducting angels. God has empowered each of us individually and collectively to manage the circumstances of life. It is our **reasonable service** to utilize that which God has provided. It is our task to avail ourselves of and accept God's wisdom, love, and power to accomplish our purpose, execute our task, and correct our karma. With the truth and spirit of God resonating in every realm and within everything, we are to prepare ourselves for the battles of life. We are to cultivate our divine nature along with the other aspects of our being so that we can be more than conquerors.

The seven archangels listed are noted with their planetary influence, associated color/ray, and the related body part/function. The wise truth student will avail him or herself of their divine influence and administration.

SEVEN ARCHANGLES

Archangel	Planet	Charka	Week Day	Color/Ray	
Michael (Who is like God, Image of God)	Sun	Crown of head (purple)	Sunday	Gold, Red, white	Heart, spine, Pineal
Gabriel (Strength of God/Man of God)	Moon	Forehead (indigo)	Monday	Blue, Silver	Breast, Fluids, reproduction system, Pituitary gland
Raphael (God Heals)	Mercury	Throat (Blue)	Wednesday	Yellow,	Nervous system, Respiratory system Thyroid gland
Haniel (Grace or Love of God)	Venus	Heart (Green)	Friday	Green	Muscles, Thymus
Khamael (Desire of God/ Burning of God)	Mars	Solar plexus (Yellow)	Tuesday	Red	Blood, Liver, Excretory system Adrenal
Tzadkiel (Righteousness of God)	Jupiter	Navel (orange)	Thursday	Purple	Stomach, Spleen, Pancreas
Tzaphkiel (Contemplation of God, God's Observation)	Saturn	Root (Red)	Saturday	Indigo	Skeleton system, Marrow

Verse 6:

In the light of God's healing power, my strength of being and purpose are invigorated and I radiate joy and confidence in living a life of vitality and virtue.

God is the strength and the joy of our lives. We are strengthened to the task that we are called or purposed, and in which we serve fallen humanity."

When we engage in "the work" in the manner that is our purpose for the present incarnation, our soul is strengthened. For such a one draws from and is connected with life energy and the hierarchy of heaven.

One's spiritual work goes to unfold and free the soul of the **negative particles/energies of mal-karma**. The **task of one's soul** may not always be obviously spiritual. It may be, and often is, associated with a career or chosen occupation. A person's job often has an *affinity* with his or her spiritual task. It is the necessary work of the soul through which one finds liberty while serving others. When one is appropriately connected with the right occupation or career it becomes a labor of love. It is not that one does not have the challenges that will aid in the process of unfolding the innate spiritual nature and soul liberty, but the sense of worth and purpose far exceeds the troubling moments. A career can serve as the means through which one finds the joy of cultivating the garden of his/her soul resulting in the fruition of the inner life.

There are a number of individuals who are unhappy with their careers or jobs because, not only does it fail to have an affinity with the compassion or purpose of their souls, it does not meet the requirements of their karma. Once disconnected from the earthly tasks that would align one with the needs of his or her soul, one does not draw the spiritual life essence that would be flowing into his or her being. Many have been coerced into pursuing careers for its monetary rewards and prestige, only to later discover dissatisfaction and the absence of fulfillment in that career path. This is not to suggest that there are some that must endure their career due to negative karmic debts. Few have avoided those jobs and situations necessary to ultimately prepare them for the right career.

A *virtuous life* is one that is *aligned with the principles of truth* and **not a religious cultural tradition** that no longer supports individual wellbeing, life purpose, or the soul's mission. Some traditions have lost their usefulness due to the changes in the state of man. The great master, Jesus, stated that "in vain do you worship me, teaching for doctrine the traditions of men." (Matthew 15:9) Virtue is the strength and nobility of character that improves one's destiny. It not only aides in the development of a healthy body and mind, but improves one's life experiences. *Virtue* that springs from within integrates one with the higher forces of heaven. The *virtuous life* is a life of righteousness, that is, the right and wise way of doing, accomplishing, and not entangling one's self or others in unnecessary mal-karma and suffering. The *virtuous life* is the caliber of existence that attracts angels, good fortune, and the favor of heaven. The foundation of *virtue*–divine truth and divine love–merits the degree of sainthood.

The emitting of *divine virtue* (power) from within yields **good health, happiness, harmony, and holiness** for others. Vice and vanity do not esteem truth, but focus on selfish endeavors that are empty. Neither vice or vanity are enduring. In time, the vanity and vices will come to haunt and trouble those who pursue such low values.

We are in the light of God's presence when we are doing that which the hierarchy of God purposed for our lives. As with the angels, our service provides healing for members of humanity. In our soul task, we are invigorated and find joy. Our confidence usually comforts those who benefit from our attuned soul nature.

Verse 7:

My health is nurtured with love and is maintained by remaining steadfast to God's perfect plan, divine truth and worthy goals.

Love essentially means to do and think only good towards another. Divine Love is the highest commandment: "Love the Lord your God with all your heart, with all your mind, with all your soul, and with all your strength, and to love thy neighbor as thyself" (Luke 10:27).

Divine Love of the true self is the prerequisite to the holy love of others. One who loves self must understand what true self is and is not. This foundation of love must be inclusive of *the mission of life and the goal of the soul.* If one truly understands, and is sentient to his or her soul, then such a one can relate to the needs and struggles of other souls in the journey of life. The *sentient soul being* must fill his or her being with *divine love* and send that *holy love* to other souls who are tangled in the web of carnality. *Love* is to envision and act towards the good of others. *Love* is caring and energizing to those who are the recipient of such noble affection. *Love* creates only good.

True love is often confused with craving, lust, possessiveness, selfishness, aggrandizement, self ingratiation, and appetites of the carnal propensities. **Carnal love** can be destructive. It likens to a predatory lion's love of sheep. A love that consumes the sheep and feeds the lions—which is carnal love at its worst—is one sided, has ill intentions, and is based on carnal emotions that can only fulfill self satisfaction. Carnal love is often so blind that it fails to perceive the ill premise of its affection and may be willing to die, kill, or both, based on its erroneous love. *True Love that is fused with divinity* is a positive and productive energy. The love that nurtures is divine and ennobling.

Love strengthens, regenerates, and revitalizes; it gives life. Love is a light that imparts harmonizing, healing energies. True love supports the purpose of life and the mission of the soul. True love of self, of one's mate, heirs, friends or associates, and/or holy order should be predicated upon these aforementioned principles, upon the **actualization of the Soul and the mission of life.**

Each organ of the physical body can be charged with the *living light of love* that springs from the *inner eye of the soul—the true light* of every man. Recognition of the organs as vessels of the spirit is the proper first step to filling and nurturing each with the rays of light, life, and love.

True Love is steadfast and does not falter during adverse and discordant circumstances. One's love for the perfect plan is the steadfastness required to encompass achievement in this life and in lives to come. This love state slows and restricts the egression of old age, which enables one to maintain vitality and youthfulness. *Love of Divine Truth* represents one's steadfastness to eternal principles as it is written: "Ye that cling to the Lord thy God are alive, every one of you this day" (Deuteronomy 4:4). *Clinging* is unwavering *love of the Divine*. Clinging to God is clinging to truth and life. Such a relationship with the Divine represents the *highest health* or *salvation state, of body, mind, and soul.*

Verse 8:

Through Christ I release stress and develop my health by exercising my being with sincere prayer, positive thinking, affirmations of truths, meditations, noble deeds, supportive acts of charity, spiritual treatments, beneficial physical exercise, and wholesome holy living.

Stress, its accompanying anxieties, and mal-emotional states are root causes of many illnesses and diseases of the body. Human circumstances and experiences can be most stressful when one lacks the resources, or is unaware and fails to apply principles that empower him or her to master the situation.

The stresses of earthly life affect our human state of being until we take dominion over the higher functions of the mind and the soul's qualities. ***Sincere prayer*** is when light emanates from our ***souls*** (the *light being within*) and our mind, and enter into the higher vibratory spheres of heaven. If the prayer is in accordance with the Divine principle (truth) and the karmic state of those involved, and if the soul/mind being is sentient, he or she will be aware of the light emanating from heaven in answer to his or her prayer.

Positive thinking involves focusing on what is desirable rather than worrying about possible negative outcomes. In the case of healing, the thoughts are to be regulated and imagined in order to create a desirable outcome. Energy follows thought. Your imagination is the mold into which the creative clay (primary energy/substance) is poured. It also entails realizing the good in adversity, and if necessary, creating "good" from hardship, difficulty, and misfortune. ***Affirmations of truth*** are keys words or phrases that reinforce personal and environmental vibrations and create the desired circumstance to manifest. Affirmation is making statements, decrees, or declarations in speech and/or thoughts that are in accordance with the will and principle of God. Divines Names, words of power, and/or mantra are effective means to initiate the kind of energy that will bring forth healing vibrations. The centurion requested that Jesus send his word. Abraham called those things that "be not, as if they were" (Romans 4:17).

The other side of endowment of *prophecy* is one who is endued to decree a thing into being. Elijah decreed that it would not rain and later prayed for the rain to come. Affirmation need not be used to try to convince others. Sometimes when others doubt and dispute one's affirmation, faith is lost; the affirmation is depleted of the energy of the soul and mind. In addition, there are adverse negative charges from the ones who resist or doubt the manifestation of the affirmation.

Silence and secrecy are often the best fields for fruition. ***Noble deeds and supportive acts of charity*** are effective means of creating the kind of karma that will release and permit, in a merciful manner, the redemption of mal-karma. By performing deeds of loving kindness, negative karma is softened. In turn, beneficial karma is created. Noble deeds and charitable acts are applicable to the deliverance of others from their afflictions and creating productive personal karma.

Charity is an act of love. When performed, charitable acts enlighten not only the hearts of its providers, but its recipients. These acts also serve to ennoble the mind and heart of others who become or are aware of the unselfish acts. Giving is not charitable (unselfish act of love) unless its purpose is to uplift the recipient. Nor is it charitable when the giver seeks recognition for his deed, gift or support. It is strange, but true, that some people need to look down on others in order to think well of themselves. This gives them a false sense of nobility. If ever that person seeks to rise, the giver feels threatened, challenged, or betrayed. One is noble because the spirit of Christ reigns within him, not because he reigns over his fellow man. The *nobility* sought is the **"crown of light" (highest charkra/thousand petal lotus)** that serves to make one a life-giving spirit with all the rights and privileges of a Christed-being. This includes healing, teaching, and uplifting fallen humanity.

Spiritual treatment entails methods and means about which volumes can be written. Spiritual treatments are means to create, enhance, or annul. These treatments can be used to heal, unfold, elevate, protect, prosper, obtain, enhance, etc. Spiritual treatments can be purely mental, emotional, ritual, physical acts, or any combination thereof. Methods of spiritual treatments include evocation, affirmations, mantra, meditations, concentration, and acts of the imagination. Jesus the Christ used several means to heal: spiritual bath, baptismal, washing in a lake seven times, marching round a building until it falls, spitting onto clay and then placing it over a man's eyes–who had been sightless from birth–to have his blindness washed away in the Pool of Siloam. Many ministers and churches or holy orders enact ceremonial magic-rituals, which are Spiritual treatments. Spiritual treatments involve the utilization of one of man's greatest powers: the power of thought. And as it has been alluded to, energy follows thought.

Beneficial physical exercise is essential to the body maintaining, healing, and sustaining health. Muscular exercise is beneficial in a number of ways. It helps relieve stress, augment one's appearance, supports physical structure, and permits one to engage in physical activities at enhanced or superior levels. It also aids in youthfulness and vitality. Oversized muscles are not always ideal, in that they take blood from other internal organs.

The exercises that promote enhanced *muscle* tone along with the *internal organs* are those that contribute more significantly to health. It is not always necessary to exercise hard but it is always essential to exercise smart. Exercise can be simple or complex, but it is best to choose the type of regimen suitable for one's temperament, and, more importantly, needs. There are several physical exercise techniques beneficial to the muscles and the internal organs. They also relieve stress, aid in mental development, regulate one emotionally, and greatly enhance spiritual unfolding.

Some exercise techniques, or approaches, are better suited for youth, while other methods can be beneficial to those who are advanced in age or compromised physically. Choose wisely. Exercise should be a scheduled part of living. There are a number of possibilities that include: power or regular-paced walking, Tai Chi, Chi Gong, Kung Fu, Aikido (or other martial arts form), yoga, divine postures, resistance training, forms of dance, Pilates, and calisthenics. Along with positive exercising is *relaxation and rest*. If one works on a level that is physical or engages in regular exercise, rest and relaxation must become a priority, as it has a substantial impact on human health and development. Sleep is a requirement of the soul as well as necessity for the body, mind, and emotions. *Sleep is a period of regeneration*. While one dreams, his mind can be instructional, prophetic, and become open to various types and kinds of revelations.

Some people go to sleep and still wake without feeling rested or regenerated. Stress can prevent one from having a normal regenerated period of sleep. In such cases, one needs to prepare by *releasing negative perceptions, internal stresses, and physical tension* before attempting to sleep. Practice positive affirmations, sincere prayer, breathing exercises, inspirational music, etc. to replace anxieties. **Rest that regenerates** can also be derived from meditation as well as a change in setting or location. The benefits of traveling to another location are due to the impact of the change in vibration. Cultural experiences, inspiring lectures or sermons, reading a good book, boating, fishing, listening to uplifting or soothing music, or an enjoyable recreational activity are effective means of obtaining rest, de-stressing and regenerating. Exercises found in such holistic forms as Tai Chi and yoga can be a means to rest and regeneration that will benefit the whole being or composite self. Rest and regeneration can be achieved through herbal baths, massage, or in state of conscious that has realized "to be still and know that God is God" (Psalm 46:10).

Wholesome holy living means that the body is respected as the Temple of the soul. The physical structure and internal organs are recognized as vessels of light and repository of life energy. Fluids, secretions, and blood flow enhance, affect, and alter consciousness and health. *Wholesome holy living* means that one will live harmoniously with nature, the cosmos, and the hierarchy of heaven. *Wholesome holy living* means to hold the spirit/soul of one's being in the highest esteem. It is a constitution and covenant with self for self, to establish, enhance, energize, equip, and exercise every aspect of one's being. It is an alliance of the composite self to wed and function harmoniously in oneness on every realm of existence. It is a testament and commitment to do no harm; to neither hamper nor hype the functions, systems, or organs of the body-temple or the body-temple of others.

Wholesome holy living means having a fulfilled life; aiding others by example and making a conscious effort to do the same. This type of life degrades none and respects all. It involves sharing and caring to impact noble possibilities and potential for one's neighbor, the world upon and the cosmos in which all beings live. *Wholesome holy living* encourages enterprising efforts that enhance the wellbeing of humanity, provides positive productivity, and renders compassionate service.

Wholesome holy living also means that the truth and the spirit of God are treasured within each individual. Work cooperatively with the hierarchy of heaven and foster positive relationships with those met along the pathways of life. Cherish the health, happiness, and harmony of the earth, cosmos, the holy order, community and neighbors. Investigate, appreciate, and respect the spirit of God within all things, all people, all cultures, and all religions.

Verse 9:

I immerse myself in the healing rays of Christ and radiate the light of health to those I meet on the pathway of life.

Every person has the potential to ignite the light of Christ to such a degree that it emanates rays–though invisible to the natural eyes–that will have healing affects on those who receive the emission of this energy. The fact that the true perception and ultimate state of the entity-man is a being of light cannot be stated enough. The phrase *man as a being of light* is difficult for many to comprehend because they walk by sight and not by a faith predicated on the truth. Their perception of life is something that begins and ends with the body and its cycles of birth and death. Some have yet to understand that the soul preexisted its physical incarnation, and also post exists the departure from the physical body, and shall return unto God. The soul will return to human existence until such experiences and states of being are no longer necessary. That is, when such a soul has become the light that GOD created it to be. It was for this reason that Jesus said to his disciplines: "You are the light of the world" (Matthew 5:14).

The life story of Jesus reflects the principle, process, and pattern of light. At the *birth* of the baby Jesus, the light is seen hovering above him. At the *baptism* of Jesus, we see the light descend upon him, entering into and remaining in his being. While at the *transfiguration,* we see that he is glorified by the light that was always with him. And the light increased in its radiant beauty and shone from within and about him like the noonday sun that indeed changed Jesus' countenance.

It is man's task to bathe and immerse in the Emanuel light, or, the light that departed from the *entities (the group Soul, Adam and Eve)* due to the infiltration of discordance vibration of duality represented by the tree of the Knowledge of Good and Evil. Oftentimes when one is angry, intoxicated, or infiltrated with negativity, evil thoughts, or mal-feelings, he or she then commits an act of abnormal behavior. It is then said that one has "lost his head." This is the present state of humanity (fallen man shattered as a group and separated as individual souls who are lost or were disconnected from the light of their divinity). Such is the present state of humanity, which has died to the spiritual existence or state of being, yet seemingly alive and well according to the carnal life. As Paul said, "to be carnally minded is death" (Romans 8:6). Having their "consciousness sheared," they are unable to perceive the light and many are lost in the world of material existence.

To those who have and are overcoming, who may have an inkling of the grand plan, it behooves them to empty themselves of their false perceptions and erroneous teachings. Purify their ignoble and wanton desires, restrict their vain and wicked ways, and reclaim the *light* of their being. Walk in the ways of wisdom.

Verse 10:

Christ is the authority that emanates health and healing within me, and is a living flame that shields me from every form of sickness, disease, disorder, and danger.

How did Jesus and the great masters of light perform their miracles and healings so effortlessly? It was due to the power of dominion that returned to them as they received the spirit/soul of the highest self. Having received the holy breath (spirit)–the maternal aspect of divinity and or the soul–they were then able to bring forth the Christ of their being. They had the authority of the Christ spirit. They evolved from a living soul that requires constant nurturing of various aspects of their beings. They obtained the state of "a life-giving spirit." Thus, people—the true essence of life that is light—have dormant in them what was obtained and manifested: authority over sickness, disease, and yes, even death.

Each one is a being capable of becoming the incarnation of light. Every being owns the potential to inherit the true light, thus being transformed into a son of God. "Beloved, now are we the sons of God, and have not manifested what you shall be, but we know that when he manifest, you shall be like him, and you shall perceive him as he is" (I John 3:2-3). "Ye are gods, but ye shall die like men" (Psalm 82:7) until we fully realize and actualize our innate divinity. "Return unto me and I will return unto you" (Malachi 3:7). "Be ye Holy for I am Holy" (I Peter 1:16). "Be ye perfect even as your father in heaven is perfect" (Matthew 5:48). The *authority of Christ frees one from all that is not holy or is imperfect.*

To the degree that we can be infused with the light of Christ, we can be healed and heal others. The intensity of this holy light will shield and protect us from disease, entities, and evil individuals. May we magnify and glorify the light of the inner Christ spirit.

The Temple of the Indwelling Christ

My body is the Temple of GOD and the SPIRIT OF GOD indwells my body. Every part of me is an instrument of divine spirit. I am wonderfully made and divinely conceived in the image of GOD. Every organ, every gland, every tissue, every cell, and every atom of my body is filled with the light of the CHRIST SPIRIT. The life and substance of my body is the WORD OF GOD made flesh.

Divine intelligence governs and regulates every activity and function of my body. The ETERNAL LIGHT OF CHRIST constantly renews and improves my body's cells, systems, structure, and functions to create health, youth, and vitality.

The blood, secretions, and fluids of my body are filled with the SPIRIT OF LIFE, LIGHT, and LOVE. The fluids, secretions, and blood are the rivers of life within my body. My fluids are never unbalanced. The secretions within me are appropriated in proportion, to serve my wellbeing and needs. My blood flows unimpeded with the light and breathe of the SPIRIT to eradicate all sickness and disease. The blood of CHRIST WITHIN me is the source of life, health, and strength.

My heart is the cup of the SPIRIT OF CHRIST. My heart is synchronized with the rhythm of the universe. It is immersed in truth and understanding. It radiates with love and sends particles of light to every organ, system, and tissue to dispel all diseases, infirmities, afflictions, mal-functions, deficiencies, accumulations, impurities, false growths, deteriorations, infections, injuries, and darkened conditions.

The life, light, and love of CHRIST maintain and ever restore my body to health. The redeeming CHRIST SPIRIT harmonizes the relationship with my physical, ethereal, astral, mental and spiritual existence. The systems of my body function in harmony with the laws of the universe, with nature, and the **INDWELLING CHRIST SPIRIT**. I am the perfect expression of health.

THE TEMPLE OF THE INDWELLING CHRIST
COMMENTARY

Verse 1:

My body is the Temple of GOD and the SPIRIT OF GOD indwells my body. Every part of me is an instrument of divine spirit. I am wonderfully made and divinely conceived in the image of GOD. Every organ, every gland, every tissue, every cell and every atom of my body is filled with the light of the CHRIST SPIRIT. The life and substance of my body is the WORD OF GOD made flesh.

Have you ever thought of your organs as habitats for angels–as vessels of light? In your Father's house there are many mansions (John 14:2) and since you are created in God's image and likeness, so too, do you have many mansions within your composite being including the physical body, the astral body, the mental body and the aspects of your soul. The organs, cells, fluids and systems of the body have a physical function but they also have a spiritual purpose.

The physical body is an instrument of light, a vessel of the spirit, a chamber containing urns of truth. When we make this inner connection with the principles of truth lodged in each respective organ, in the fluids, in secretions, in cells, etc. of our being, we are awakening and aligning with the source of life. This inner connection with the principles of truth is our spiritual task. We make this inner connection through our meditations, through the evocations of our soul, through breathing in the breath of life and through our harmonious right actions.

As we properly feed the physical organ of our being with wholesome food, and as we learn how to nurture the inner aspects of the spirit therein with positive life energy (Prana, Chi, Ki, etc.), we can renew ourselves. We increase our days and become more effective *Living Temples of God*. There are a number of systems or methods that will actualize this potential–such as silent meditation, moving mediations, breath of life techniques, divine postures & gestures, affirmations, sacred sounds, chants, singing spiritual songs, mantras, divine names, etc.–which should always be accompanied with thoughts and feeling ennobled by sacred truth.

The body and all of its components are the garden that you are to cultivate. The tools needed to maintain and beautify the garden of the soul are the mind, the will, imagination, concentration, meditation, love and truth. It would be hard to imagine a gardener or agriculturist (farmer) pouring sodas, alcohol and other beverages of such ill-content into a garden or field that he/she had planted. A good gardener or farmer nurtures the plants and fields–enabling them to grow and be strong. The task of cultivating a life existence that will be purposeful and fulfilling must include the principles of truth in each area and/or aspect of our lives.

"[You] are wonderfully made" (Psalm 139:14) because you are the substance of truth. The essence of your being is composed of the WORD. In the kabbalah and scriptures of the Judaic-Christian faith, the WORD is the composite of the Aleph-Beths. Obtaining this true conscious perception of self is essential and will greatly aid one in obtaining the energy/substance, and thereby transform and transfigure one's being. Health, as with all aspects of life, must have a vision. Indeed without a vision, we perish. All need the courage and love to use one's will, imagination and mediations to visualize the desired health results. The "perceptive means of treatment" to sustain health, eradicate disease and align our being with all the beneficial virtues of every realm of existence, can have a dynamic affect on one's whole health and/or healing of the composite self.

There are many accounts, as well as statistical data, that indicate it is very much within the capacity of the individual to positively or negatively affect health and disease. The images that one uses to counteract the development of a disease, or to eliminate it, are based on the commitment and the esteem given to the "thought forms" created as the power source to affect healing and restoration.

Many of the biochemical reactions in the body are initiated by the intensity and by the persistent thought and feeling of the thinker. "As a man thinketh, so he is" (Proverbs 23:7) and "what I have feared has come upon me" (Job 3:25) are axioms that reveal the power and affects of one's thinking upon one's self.

The Taoist has identified the positive virtues and ill vices that can lodge in our organs. There are wonderful meditative treatments and physical exercises to improve the health, aid in eliminating the negative vices and increase strength, as well as improve the state of the organs inner purpose and function.

The body like the Hebrew temple has three chambers: the outer court corresponding with the pelvic area, the inner court or Holy place corresponds to the chest chamber and the holy of holies denotes the skull. There is nothing in the temple that is not reflected in the physical body of man. Paul, being a kabbalist, knew this. The body is indeed the temple not built with hands.

Verse 2:

Divine intelligence governs and regulates every activity and function of my body. The ETERNAL LIGHT OF CHRIST constantly renews and improves my body's cells, systems, structure and functions to create health, youth, and vitality.

This is the problem: light has come into the world, and men love darkness. Enthralled by the senses and selfish desires of vanities, plagued by vices of the temporal nature, inhibited by doubts of a carnal mind, man effectively refuses, ignores, disregards, disbelieves and blocks out the divine influence.

This verse decrees and confirms that through man's volition, he yields his composite being to the authority of Divine intelligence. In this way, the function of the various systems and the activities of every organ, gland, tissues, along with every secretion, fluid, and cell are under the governance of divine intelligence. Man, desirous of this state of being, must be cooperative and in alliance with the higher intelligence. There should be little fear in doing so, as the great master indicated: "take my yoke upon you ... for my yoke is easy and my burden is light" (Matthew 11:29-30).

The entrance of the Christ light spirit into every aspect of one's being is the path to freedom and fulfillment. The *eternal light* is the *deathless, unlimited energy source* that is more than capable of renewing, regenerating and improving the body on the cellular level of every system, every function, and the structure to the very marrow of the bones. This vitalization by divine light goes to create health, youth, and vitality for the individual. By way of genetics, longevity has been passed on to some because of the predisposition of their DNA's ancestry. However, this divine intelligence can improve the code of life to express the design and intent of divinity of the primordial man –the son of God. As Jesus and other master have demonstrated in their lives, it is indeed possible to be transfigured by light.

Verse 3:

The blood, secretions, and fluids of my body are filled with the SPIRIT OF LIFE, LIGHT, and LOVE. The fluids, secretions, and blood are the rivers of life within my body. My fluids are never unbalanced. The secretions within me are appropriated in proportion to serve my well-being and needs. My blood flows unimpeded with the light and breathe of the SPIRIT to eradicate all sickness and disease. The blood of CHRIST WITHIN is the source of life, health, and strength.

Every organ and all aspects of man's being have conscious life. This is most true of the blood, as is written in the scripture, "life is in the blood" (Leviticus 17:11). But this is equally true of the secretions of the body as well as the fluids, which as with all things, have conscious life. The highest manifestation of life is light. The highest expression of life is love. In the challenges of life it is most important to have balance. As it relates to the blood, fluid, and secretion, one must sustain *a balance that is appropriate for the task*. The flow of light, life, and love are necessary to overcome the dark emotions that would leave one helplessly drowning in doubt, despair, destructiveness, and depravation. It is undesirable that man's ability to discern and discriminate with the light, life, and love be flooded out by the likes of malefic feelings of anger, hate, lust, envy, and selfishness. The flow of light, life, and love is critical to enrich and make fertile man's every noble endeavor so that he is not found in a state of being destitute of the eternal true reality with its wisdom, love, and power.

This verse of the affirmation decrees and invites the mind and body *consciousness* into a harmonious symbiotic relationship–into a unified higher perception. The result of such will be a higher state wherein the function of the blood. The fluids, and the secretions of the body are then *rightly discerned and properly functioning as the rivers of life* (connected to, and attuned with, the higher spiritual forces—the triad of light, life, and love). Blood, as the carrier of the life elements, must be given those things that are vital to physical health. Man must have the necessary vitamins, enzymes, and minerals for his bio-chemical requirements. But they serve little purpose if they are not absorbed and assimilated into the body's system. To be sure that such assimilation occurs, ensure that the blood is kept pure and free of contaminates. It must be made certain that the organs involved in the assimilation and bio-chemical processes are properly functioning: uninhibited, and uncompromised.

The blood is reported to make a complete transformation in ninety days, which gives one an opportunity to transform his or her health within that period. Any regimen of supplements or diet aimed at improving one's health can be evaluated after a ninety-day cycle to better assess its effectiveness or lack thereof. There are times when a body is overloaded and already compromised with excessive activity and supplements.

Rather than taking a progressive approach and schedule that will allow one's systems and organs to adjust to the newness of supplements, exercise, or internal activities, one tends to strain and stress the body. A more effective approach is to cleanse the system prior to adding supplements as a systematic plan. Then continue the treatment and/or supplements for ninety days, allowing for the transformation of the blood. Some failures are due to overloading a system that is ill-prepared to effectively assimilate the nutritional level imposed. The body simply eliminates what it cannot manage.

An additional failure is when one discontinues the needed treatment due to the lack of immediate and similar results and desired expectations: a response that likens to that of drug stimulants or depressants. Organic products and treatment works in a steady, gradual manner but also maintains its results for a longer period. In general, the organic products result in a cure that is not only effective but does not have negative side effects when properly administered. Finding the right supplements or products for a body to absorb is key. Some hard tablets are not assimilated and pass through the body in the same form in which it was ingested. Capsules are generally better at being digested, while liquids such as juices, beverages, and herbal teas readily absorb into the system. The body must also be supplied with its required enzymes in order to build and nurture itself. Enzymes are key to the assimilation and transformation of the body, and greatly aids in healing and health.

It is most essential that glands function in a positive manner, because they are undeniably required for the transformations, physical activities, life functions, and conditions needed to maintain health and promote healing. Wellness, expressiveness, and appropriateness (physically, mentally and emotionally) all rely on the proper secretion of glands and organs.

The endocrine glands are essentially miniature brains (in composition) within the body that provide internal ductless secretions into the bloodstream. They are specialized workmen, each with expert abilities. Each has specific functions that aid the body in various physical processes, functions, and needs. The *seven* primary endocrine glands are the pineal, pituitary, thyroid and parathyroid, thymus, adrenal, pancreatic, and the testes or ovaries. They are the physical correspondents of the *seven* churches depicted in Revelations, as well as the focal points of the seven major chakras revealed in the *kundalini* yoga system. *Ecclesia*, the Greek word for church, means "called out." And it is these glands that are called out and physically emit directly into the body's bloodstream.

These glandular secretions, separately and in combinations, have an effect on the physical body, emotional states, and mental dispositions. They are regulators within the body and this affirmation is a decree for each ductless gland, duct gland, and organ's secretions to be governed by the Divine Spirit of light, life, and love. This affirmation decrees the infusion of the highest directly into the blood, fluids, secretions, tissues, and organs of one's body temple, thereby reigning supreme. It is a proclamation of the higher self to align with the lesser nature to maintain balance in the operation of the physical and metaphysical. This decree proclaims that the secretions of both the ductless and duct systems, along with every biochemical process and action of the organs, function in a manner appropriate for the array of life experiences including physical health and healing, stimulating the appropriate mental and emotional states, expanding of the mind, and unfolding of the soul.

When directed by our elevated and spiritualized will, proper prayer and meditation will alter our state of consciousness and connect us with the life energies that aids in healing and health maintenance. The state of mind that results from true prayer and divine meditation has a positive, stimulating effect on the endocrine or spiritual centers of the body. When done wisely, directed meditations on these centers can be most beneficial.

Visualization of light as the governing Christ-force of the activities of the glands, secretions, fluid, and blood, harmonizes us with the accompanying life and love principle that enriches our existence and removes the negative and darkened conditions from our transcendental bodies. This results in the manifestation of healing and health within our physical being. This verse in this affirmation is a *decree* to obtain the knowledge and accompanying intelligence needed–along with the inner forces of light, life, and love needed–to guide, enrich, and empower one to maintain a state of composite health that leads to a wholesome holy life.

Verse 4:

My heart is the cup of the SPIRIT OF CHRIST. My heart is synchronized with the rhythm of the universe. It is immerged in truth and understanding. It radiates with love and sends particles of light to every organ, system, and tissue to dispel all diseases, infirmities, afflictions, mal-functions, deficiencies, accumulations, impurities, false growths, deteriorations, infections, injuries, and darkened conditions.

The heart, with its four arteries and chambers, is symbolic of the four rivers in the story of the Garden of Eden and as such is synchronized with the intent, purpose, and possibilities of those streams. This synchronization is not of the highest level, nonetheless, its potential is worthy of every effort made. Our archeologist and geologist have long sought to discover these rivers upon the planet earth and may have found or will find the earth's *facsimile*. However, the rivers along with the vast majority of the *creation* and *fall* tales of the **Adamites** (the **composite group souls** now known as the *individualized separated souls* called "fallen humanity or *shattered lights*") are *metaphysical stories* that deal in principles related to an adventure in higher states of existence. This tale of the Adamites is one that took place in a higher sphere of existence.

The Adamites (Adam and Eve), after undergoing sin and shame, had the opportunity to admit or confess the errors of their ways and to purify (baptize) themselves in the rivers of Eden. This is suggested in the scripture prior to the fall. Lacking the integrity to do so, each in turn placed the blame outside of themselves and indicated that the fault was not their own. The *masculine being, Adam,* not only placed the fault on Eve, but included God by saying it "was the woman that you [***God***] gave me" (Genesis 3:12). Eve, the feminine being, in turn blamed *Satan* for her misdeed of choosing his misrepresented perspective (an admixture of truth and lies) over the direction of the Divine. Satan had no one to blame for his treachery, but had little or no plausible cause to **beguile** the children of God. Nonetheless, it is the satanic being that is said to be the great accuser of man in his misdeeds not only to God, but to each individual.

What Adam and Eve should have done was to acknowledge their wrongs and not attempt to excuse themselves by placing blame elsewhere: *confess the sin.* The law of the universe is just: You shall reap what you have sown (Galatians 6:7). Lying will not make things better, only mercy and repentance—a change of mental perception and accompanying committed actions. Sin or mal-karma is not as subjective as superficial minds will have one believe. The substance of sin or mal-karma is "energy particles." It hibernates within one's existence and explodes in experiences and/or crystallizes as obstacles and shears to his or her health, happiness, harmony, and holiness. Sin (mal-karma), as Paul wrote, is within. As energy, entities, or forces, it impels one to wrongdoing and forestalls good deeds. If not properly corrected, neutralized, or eradicated, sin can be dangerous as well as deadly to various levels of one's being, both physically and metaphysically. The committing of sin is assuredly misleading man from one ill concept, or, ill state, to his ultimate death or life situations on the wheel of sorrow.

This lying to the Divine, as it is with lying to self, is a great sin. As a result of this mal-karmic act of perjury, man lost the true perception of his higher nature (the seed of divinity) as well as his access and presence in the higher realm. God seeks those who will worship him in spirit and in truth. (John 4:24) Certainly one sees the need for unadulterated truth, which is vital to true contemplation and actualization of the innate divinity of man along with the right relationship with God. Pure lies, truth mixed with lies, or truths ill perceived are the major causes of all mankind's dilemmas.

One can reclaim and actualize his/her divinity. To do so he/she must purify both the mind and heart; remove the erroneous perceptions that give birth, form, and habitation to inharmonious and evil thought-forms and emotional entities of the heart that results in the further creation of negative, mal-karmic energy-particles. This is accomplished through the confession of one's errors and the affirmation of truth in thoughts, words, and deeds.

Purification of the heart is as essential to health as it is to the actualization of the soul. The heart is the center and circuit of love and the distributor of life, in its higher function. Yet, it can be, and all too often is, a container of a plethora of putrid emotions contradictive and adversarial to love and courage. Adversarial entities of emotional and mental thought-forms must be dispelled from the heart and from all organs. That is to remove the *spell*, the beguilement, and mesmerized state that has man attached to vanities, vices, vengeful, vicious behavior, and erroneous perceptions. Man is to dispel—drive out of the temple of health, happiness, harmony and holiness—the enemies that cause discontent with his covenant with nature, the cosmos, and the hierarchy of heaven.

Verse 5:

The life, light, and love of CHRIST maintain and ever restore my body to health. The redeeming CHRIST SPIRIT harmonizes the relationship with my physical, ethereal, astral, mental and spiritual existence. The systems of my body function in harmony with the laws of the universe, with nature, and the INDWELLING CHRIST SPIRIT. I am the perfect expression of health.

Salvation is not in part, but in whole. The ideal state of existence is a fivefold alliance, wherein man's composite self is in accordance with his spirit/soul being. This does not mean that man will not wrestle with challenges, but that he will have connection with the light, the life, and love of Christ to ever restore and redeem him.

Perfect health, or, complete health, is the synchronization of each aspect of one's being into an integrated unit, properly realigned and functioning as God intended. Once realigned with the Christ of man's being, the composited self functions as one entity that maintains and restores the physical existence in a harmonious relationship with nature, the cosmos, and the hierarchy of heaven.

Healing Light

I thank thee, O Living God of healing, for the understanding that I am a being of light and for the true perception that the body is a vessel of light.

I realize that it is essential to my spiritual existence, growth, elevation and unfoldment that I be nurtured by the spectrum of light.

The True Light of my being shall serve to eliminate and extinguish the darkness of negativity and disease. The spectrum of light stimulates and strengthens radiant health for every aspect of my composite existence. The spectrum of light emanates it healing and harmonizing vibrant colors to my affairs and multi-folded nature.

I shall constantly purify and invigorate my inner being in the spectrum of light's energy-waves of healing and harmony. I envision these energy waves circulating its rays of light, descending from the crown of my head to each center of energy-consciousness in the front and back of me. Waves of energy traverse through the five meridians from the crown of by head to the sole and toes of my feet.

From the eternal Kingdom of God's Infinite Living Light, I am united with the Divine Mind to create the colors—the vibratory waves of light energy—that shall result in my restoration and regeneration.

Divine Light has the brilliance and the radiant power to heal. I work harmoniously with the brilliance and the emanating power of light to bring the vibrant colors I need to restore and renew my life energy.

The spectrum of colors from the treasury of light creates and manifests the power that I desire and need to bring forth harmonious results. Color is a manifestation of divine intelligence and angelic power that is readily available to restore health, happiness, harmony and holiness.

Light is the primary energy-substance of the Infinite that created me, and is the same supreme source, eternal power and absolute authority that heals me. As I visualize, I actualize from the eternal source—the supreme unlimited holy power that shall free me, and restore me to harmony, happiness and health.

Silently and assuredly, I know and allow the great healing process to achieve the goal of harmony and health for my fourfold existence. I praise and rejoice with an inner smiles as the healing light transforms, preserves and creates within my spiritual/energy centers health and holiness that results in wholeness and true salvation.

I apply the color to the spiritual energy centers, and as I do, each center is now awaken and charged to perform and produce in the manner designed by the Divine Plan of God.

HEALING LIGHT
COMMENTARY

Let There Be Light!

In him was life and the life was the light of men (John 1:4).

Man is a being of light. As a being of light, it is up to him to what degree he will shine or become illuminated. He has the capability to radiate and emanate healing rays that restore health. With an *illuminated soul* he can bring holiness into the world of his existence. With an *enlightened mind,* he can emanate harmonious vibratory energy that reestablishes peace and balance as he disseminates the unadulterated truth.

With *a radiant heart of love,* he can emit rays of happiness and bliss. With *a body energized and infused with light,* he can vanquish the darkness of disease, depravation, dysfunctional physical conditions, and death; and give light, life, and love. The cognition of one's self as a being of light brings one into a sphere of grand awareness and possibilities. It is a culture of understanding wherein one directs his/her life based on higher principles and esteemed spiritual values. *The Culture of light* empowers the mind and heart to transforms one's character and consequentially his or her destiny. This *light culture* ignites the divine spark in every aspect of one's composite existence, until such an initiate becomes one with the infinite light that illuminates the soul. *The culture of Light,* teaches one how to **cultivate the electro-magnetic centers of consciousness and power** within his or her being. The instructions elucidated in the culture of light provide the safe practices, treatments, methods and means to awaken the dynamic energy-centers of consciousness (chakras). Yet it is always guarded from those who desire power and authority without purpose and altruism. This remains hidden from those who lack truth principles (*the essence of wisdom)* and righteousness (*the right manner/right vibratory* *state).* The development of the spiritual centers is essential to one's health, happiness, harmony, and holiness.

According to science, light is defined as *electromagnetic radiation.* This electromagnetic radiation that, due to its frequency and wavelength, manifests itself in various ways including radio waves, microwave radiations, terahertz radiation, infrared radiation, visible light, ultraviolet radiation, and gamma rays. Furthermore, light travels on a straight line at a speed of 186,282 mile per second in a vacuum. It can be refracted, which has resulted in utilitarian inventions that include microscopes, telescopes, magnifying glasses, and contact lenses. Electromagnetic radiation (light) emits its energy and momentum into matter. Light as a photon has both the characteristic of energy and particles. Akin to light, man is a photonic being that has the characteristic of both energy and particles, materially and metaphysically. Light is electromagnetic, so too are man and woman. Both the genders have twofold qualities of magnetism and electricity. The male species is magnetic on the upper half of his body and electric on the lower half, while the female is electric on the upper half of her physical structure and magnetic on the lower half. This is designed for the sake of compatibility.

The nature of the genders and their functions, abilities, and services is predicated on the nature of energy and the area in which it primarily resides. Although the revelation of the polarity of the gender is a wonderful study, it is not the purpose of this text, and shall be taken up in another discourse.

The children of God must emulate the creator by declaring light into their beings, affairs, environment, as well as their health. There is no life without the energy of light. Man can live days without food and water, and minutes with the last breath of air. But without the energy of light, life ceases to exist. With divine light infused in the soul, mind, and heart of the individual, unlimited potential and supernatural manifestations are the inherent state of his or her being. The great principles of truth that are contained within the text of this affirmation offer the seeker enlightenment to elevate his or her concepts of *thought, energy,* and of the *true self*. **You are a being of light.** These principles enable the initiate to become an ***executive of light*** by drawing from and working with the properties and principles of light from the higher state of existence, thereby elevating and improving one's being and circumstances. When one becomes an executive of radiant energy, he or she will have obtained the Light that illuminates the soul and enlightens the mind. He will be infused with the light that fills him and allows him to emit emanating, enthused emotions and to radiate vibrant health within the body.

The Spectrum of Light

If light is essential to life, then *color, a property of light,* holds significance in its manifestation and greatly influences the lives of all, and certainly influences the individual. The capacity of color to infuse and influence the circumstance of life on every level of existence is worthy of meditation and in-depth study. Color is not only a thing of beauty, but also of power.

Color is creative. It can preserve as well as transform or destroy. The utilization of color is a spiritual art that can change the canvas of one's life in terms of health of the body, happiness of the heart, harmony of the mind, and holiness of the soul. Color is the manifestation of energy, emotions, and intelligence.

Light has a spectrum of colors that are both visual and invisible. Color is a means by which light distributes specific electromagnetic energies. Color is vibratory energy that within its chromatic scale begins with the lowest vibratory color of red and then ascending to orange, then higher to yellow, raising to the higher vibrating green, then advancing to blue, then elevates to indigo, and to the violet. Color is a vibration or frequency of electromagnetic radiation, and as such, can alter the vibration or frequency of one's being. The vibratory power of color can alter the consciousness, character, and circumstances of the individual. These vibratory changes can be beneficial and result in positive changes that heal and regenerate health. Color can aid in calming or stimulating one's emotional and mental state. It is a tool for spiritual transformation and soul elevation.

The application of colors has multifold uses that aid the individual in the creative process and management of life. Properly applied, color can serve to awaken and empower one to grander levels of his or her true state. Color serves to heal, protect, harmonize, prosper, energize, beatify, and unfold. Spiritually, some are not only colorblind, but chromatically color deaf and non-sentient to the vibration of colors that are the intrinsic power of light. The aura, or, the emanations emitted from the centers of consciousness and energy, reveals in its field of light one's predominated nature or state of being. Our priests or religious leaders may wear robes of loftiness spiritual significance, but their aura may indicate an entirely contradictory spiritual state. However, if the soul that dons a garment designed to channel spiritual energies in synch with his or her spiritual development, he or she will find the flow of spiritual energy more efficient and magnified. One's aura is a colored orb of light that emanates his or her true nature, status, and state of existence. It is a living light field of protection when so intensified, but it is also a vibratory radiant field of harmonizing healing, blessings, and holiness; a holy field of living lighting in which angelic beings can dwell.

Angels are beings of light and or colors; they are often thought of as corporal beings. It is true that they may manifest themselves in such a manner to communicate with, bless, and influence human beings. But they are light entities, beings of colors. Angels, depending on their degree, are emanations of single or multi-mingled colors. *Flowers* and *a class of angelic* beings are fused beings of vibratory energies that have influence, divine intelligence, and potency. It is beneficial to keep flowers around, and to cultivate its positive radiant light energy into man's existence.

The *Archangels* are associated with the *seven primary planetary principles* and works with their corresponding *colors, day of the week*, and *astrological signs*. The utilization of color's energy to work with the Archangels for healing and harmony is a simple master key to obtaining the virtue and powers of heaven, or as the Christ instructed: "Take my yoke upon you . . . for my yoke is easy, and my burden is light." (Matthew 11:29-30) The difficulty in working with spiritual treatments, prayer, and meditation is having the faith, patience, and the love to allow the inner seeds to come to fruition. Imagine a pebble falling into a still pond and not creating ripples. It is the nature of matter. In the same manner, one should imagine a prayer entering the great pond of heaven and creating rippling emanations of blessing in the form of light and colors. It is the nature of heaven. Doubt is the acidic rain upon one's field of hope, faith, dreams, and prayers; the dark hole that absorbs the light of our blessings. Fear is the ravenous dark raven that seeks to pluck from one's existence, one's blessings and one's divine rights. Fear is the dark emotional storms that shatter and scatter the energies required to gestate one's blessing. Agents of light and vibratory energies, *metals, stones*, and *gems* have both angelic properties and effects on one's aura. With the radiation of vibrant electromagnetic color, these objects infuse the atmosphere on every level including one's aura.

Stones and gems can be best perceived as gestated chromatic light. Of all the many influences on earth from which one can be aided, gems, and to a lesser degree, stones and metals are of the highest spiritual emanations. The properties of these gems, stones, and metal add electromagnetic energy that can contribute to one's health, property, protection, unfolding, dreams, and other beneficial needs. These resources are empowering and are to be used wisely. The high priest had twelve gemstones. They can be used to attract and magnify good or to repel and diminish evil, adverse forces.

When one is not certain which color should be used in healing or blessing, then white, a composite of the colors, is always appropriate. Before beginning a healing, the healer should take time in moments, minutes, or hours to assure there is a positive connection with the White Light. This not only provides one with the radiant energy necessary for healing, but it protects for the contamination of lower vibratory energies and entities that are being cast out or eradicated. The healer should always be sure that he or she has freed of any lingering ill vibration or entities.

Though all may heal, too many want undue credit for healing. It is the Light that heals. Like cooking, you may prepare a tasty nutritional meal, but it is nature via divine intelligence that brought forth every component of the meal provided. The role of the cook, like the role of the healer, is to utilize what GOD has created. The healer's role is to learn how to infuse self with light, as well as how to work with the wisdom and intelligence of the light. The emission of light and color is one of the highest methods of healing. It requires no touch. In the story of the centurion who came to ask Jesus to heal a member of his household, the centurion only wanted Jesus to send his word. He recognized Jesus' authority or mastership of the heavenly ways, and Jesus appraised the centurion's faith as being on a higher level than those he found in Israel. Although it was healing of a higher means, it mandates that the healer be empowered to emit the quality of light to heal and that the patient be receptive.

Spiritual Energy Centers of Conscious

There are a plethora of energy centers and channels within one's being. The *seven major centers* are associated with the *endocrine system* and the *nerve plexuses*. The seven centers via the Asian theological systems are distinctly known as the seven Chakras. The life force and conscious energies in these centers are reflected by the colors emanated. The book of Revelations refers to them as the "seven churches of Asia." The Greek word for church, *ekklesia* connotes an assembly or means "to be called out." The spiritual center is an assembly of thought forms and emotional entities, both of which have either a positive beneficial contribution to one's life (harmonizing existence with the hierarchy of heaven, spiritual evolvement, and soul freedom) or leads to a life of bondage, wasteful vanity & unrestricted greed, and selfishness & destruction.

Asia (as mentioned in the Book of Revelations) represents the *inner plane*, the realms where *the spiritual centers* exist. Their corresponding points of contact in the physical body are the *seven primary endocrine glands*. Each gland is associated with an archangel, planet, sound, and color.

SPIRITUAL CENTERS

Chakra / Gland	Archangel	Planet	Sound	Color
Crown / Pineal	Michael	Sun (gold, orange)	Aum	Violet
Brow / Pituitary	Gabriel	Moon (Blue, Silver)	Om	Indigo
Throat / Thyroid	Raphael	Mercury (Yellow)	Hum	Blue
Heart / Thymus	Haniel	Venus (Green)	Yam	Green
Solar plexus / Adrenal	Khamael	Mars (Red)	Ram	Yellow
Navel / Pancreatic	Tzadiel	Jupiter (Purple)	Vam	Orange
Root Ovary / Testicular	Cassiel	Saturn (Indigo)	Lam	Red

The True Light of Being

The true state of the entities called man is light, and in this text are several delineations that elucidate upon this point. MAN was *created* in the image of GOD as an entity of light. He was *formed* of the *photonic light-particle* described as *dust* and later installed in coats of skin *made* by GOD. The entity called MAN, who was a LIVING SOUL designed to evolve to a LIFE GIVING SPIRIT, lost the innate principle or seed-spirit that he was to cultivate. Recapturing this spirit of light is the goal of every thinker upon the earth.

The light that man can achieve is the task of incarnation. It is unfortunate that there are so many who are unaware. These numbers are compounded by those who have been made aware and yet reject the truth of their being along with those who are aware but do not esteem this task as their highest goal. They dare hold trivia and licentious pursuits as their avid desires and deeds.

As Jesus said: "What good is it for a man to gain the whole world, and yet lose or forfeit his very self?" (Luke 9:25). The light of the spiritual center/chakra is the emanation that creates the seven-layer aura. The predominating color of the aura is the result of the dominant function from the chakra wherein one's major thoughts and desires prevails. The predominance of the lower centers/chakras manifests as one character type and color. The color of the lower chakras is an indication of one's inability to access the higher hierarchy of heaven. Until one learns and actively applies the light to ignite the higher center, to purify and regulate the lower centers of life, he or she will continue to exist in a dysfunctional carnal state that promotes false perceptions of self and others.

The life energies of the crown chakra must purify, ennoble, and lift the energy and conscious of the lower chakras. To do otherwise would lead to unbalanced states, carnal fixation and addiction, and, ultimately, madding states wherein the true soul of one's being cannot inhabit the human vessel. The confession, baptism, and reception of the holy breath (spirit) are the ritual steps that emulate what the Adamites should have done after their disobedience of GOD's command and acceptance of the satanic perception.

Breath is spirit. Like the yoga system with its five states of prana, the Hebrew kabbalah system has five breaths, or aspects, of the soul. These aspects are descriptive perceptions of the inner levels; the highest being a divine existence. According to the kabbalah system, each breath, or soul aspect, that one connects with, brings a state of consciousness/existence and innate power that ultimately transforms one into a **life giving spirit, a Christed being, a divine soul**. Infusing the natural breath with the radiant light energy of colors is empowering on several level of existence.

Color breathing is a wonderful way to infuse light into oneself. It has the capabilities of assisting the individual in self healing, regeneration, empowerment, and awakening self to greater potential. Like other meditative techniques or physical exercises, color breathing should become an integral part of one's regimen to achieve desired results.

FIVE SPIRITUAL BREATHS

KABBALAH	COLOR
Unique Being/ Yechidah The Only Begotten	Blue
Life/ Chayah	Green
Holy breath/ Neshema	Yellow
Rational soul/ Ruach	Orange
Animal soul/ Nephesh	Red

THE KINGOM OF GOD
INFINITE LIVING LIGHT

There are varied reasons why one may be ill, or suffer. The methods to deal with the ills and suffering of humanity are as diverse as its causes. There are many who serve to the best of their ability but also with limitations to their knowledge. They assist individuals in living a quality of life wherein their conditions are managed, but not cured.

One should be thankful for those dedicated to the material medical arts and sciences of healing and health. Those who render services that harms the body or discredits true healing predominately for its monetary value should rightfully be questioned and contested.

As a patient and/or observer of care and medical providers, one cannot and should not be ignorant of the medical treatments and products received. Each individual needs a working knowledge of the body, nutrition, and of the plethora of treatments (Western and traditional) to maintain and foster his or her health and eliminate disease. To the enlightened, one should never eliminate the benefits of spiritual treatment in restoring and maintaining health.

The advance of illness, disease, and suffering needs to be recognized from the levels and sources from which it sprung and manifested in the physical body, that is, the state of one's existence or the metaphysical aspect of one's being. Spiritual treatment can be simple or complex. The simple treatments are often the best. One only needs to send his or her word, the composite of spiritual energies and principles in the form of letters, sounds, or thoughts, which are the power that creates supernaturally. For the masses, the more complex methodologies are often required and are deemed more effective. This is because the *client* requires a more direct contact to their personage to ignite the receptive aspect of their faith. Some individuals are not good receptors of spiritual or metaphysical energies.

One should be mindful that the Infinite Christ light and power to heal is ever available, remotely or directly. This power works according to how one hopes or imagines it to work with his or her perception and alignment with divinity (GOD). Healing is not always of, or for, the physical body. It is possible for a soul to depart and yet be—and sometimes thereby—healed and freed of the condition that resulted in the illness.

Harmony of the higher states of one's existence, like immortality, is not required of the physical body. Paul noted this when he said, "Which body shall you rise?" (I Corinthians 15:35) There is one glory of the terrestrial body and another glory of the celestial body. One must create, or have created, such means and conditions that will promote and render healing. Supernatural healing is the means wherein the physical is infused with the refracted or magnified light of healing. Thus the physical become magnetized with radiant light energy that increases the potency and effectiveness of the natural.

Supernatural healing can be as simple as the prayers or affirmations evoked before eating a meal, or more dynamically involved as the laying of hands on one who is ill, or the emission of highly charged spiritual thoughts radiating with light, life, and love. The master key to being effective in prayer and in spiritual treatment is to know that prayers, like thoughts, are real. Prayers that are founded on divine truth principles exist and manifest in the higher realms. Prayer radiates from the soul and the higher mind when predicated on truth, divine principle, and life's purpose. Prayers of the righteous are the most effective. This due to the righteous not only understanding and having faith in the invisible or hidden power of spirit, but the *righteous state* of existence which enables them to function better because they are more attuned and in alliance with the hierarchy of heaven and its supremacy over the lower realms. However, one cannot discount the soul sincere prayer of anyone who has the God kind of faith. Prayer in itself is an alternate state of consciousness wherein one is most effective in opening channels for divine intelligence and divine power to intervene.

The elements, serving as vessels for the kingdom of GOD, can be utilized to initiate healing. Many light candles to ignite the healing energies. Some use the air in breathing exercises, sounds, emitting a spirit-filled breath, or in words (affirmations and prayers). Others employ baptismal rites with water and/or the fluid essence from that found in nature (plants, herbs, etc.). Other instruments of the earth noted for its healing property–of which gems, stones, metal, plants, herbs are key to such treatments–are also used. The combining of the elements is also a viable means to aid in the restoration of health, happiness, harmony, and holiness.

Elements comprise the body. The appropriate balancing, utilization, and operation of the elements are essential to health. It is difficult to imagine a healthy body that would be without any one of the elements. Think for a moment of a physical body without heat or warmth, water or fluid, air or gases, or without all the component substance of the earth elements that contributes to life and health. The elements must be in appropriate proportions, or balanced chemically, to have health. It is unhealthy to have a body that is overheated or too cold. It is life threatening to have a system that only inhales, or exhales, or is overly compressed with any gaseous substance. One can imagine the horror of a body overflowing with, or depleted of, fluids. Both thirst and dehydration, and excessive intakes of water or other fluid, are deadly.

THE REALMS OF THE KINGDOM OF GOD ARE CHARACTERIZED BY THE ELEMENTS:

ELEMENTS	REALMS OF THE KINGDOM	ASPECTS OF THE SOUL
FIRE	SPIRITUAL PLANE/ WORLD OF EMANATION	LIFE
AIR	MENTALPLANE/ WORLD OF CREATION	BREATH
WATER	ASTRAL PLANE/ WORLD OF FORMATION	ASTRAL- FORM/ RATIONAL SOUL /
EARTH	PHYSICAL PLANE/ WORLD OF ACTION/MADE EVOLUTION/GESTATION	ANIMAL SOUL/ BODY

The healers can be and are great physicians of the physical body, who relieve many of the symptoms and/or actual diseases within the physical plane. Other healers operate on another transcendental level utilizing principles from the metaphysical planes.

It is a noble aspiration to want to become a healer, as long as you know that your primary client who needs to be healed is yourself. The wise philosopher, Socrates, admonished those seeking wisdom "to know thyself." In accordance with this principle of wisdom, if you are seeking to restore another's health, you are strongly advised "to heal thyself." You cannot be the solvent of healing when you are plagued and contaminated with physical illnesses, discordance attitudes, states of mental dispositions and even soul conditions that either prevents your effectiveness, farther contaminate you and/or cause problems to the individual(s) you wish to heal. Spiritual healing or energy healing requires that you have the spirit and/or energy to heal, as well as, an effective method or treatment to do so. It also entails a purifying process to eliminate or eradicate the darkened conditions or entities of the illness and/or disease. Many have sacrificed their own health and well being in their attempts to heal or bless others. One of the principles of alchemy is, that if you are going to make gold, you must have gold. Or as Peter stated, " . . . silver and gold have I none, but such as I have I give unto you." (Acts 3:6)

www.ingramcontent.com/pod-product-compliance
Lightning Source LLC
Chambersburg PA
CBHW072035060426
42449CB00010BA/2271